Self-discipline

Kimberley Jane Pryor

MACMILLAN
LIBRARY

First published in 2010 by
MACMILLAN EDUCATION AUSTRALIA PTY LTD
15–19 Claremont Street, South Yarra 3141
Reprinted 2011

Visit our website at www.macmillan.com.au or go directly
to www.macmillanlibrary.com.au

Associated companies and representatives throughout the world.

National Library of Australia Cataloguing-in-Publication entry

Pryor, Kimberley Jane, 1962–
    Self-discipline / Kimberley Jane Pryor.
    ISBN: 9781420278200 (hbk.)
    Pryor, Kimberley Jane, 1962– Values.
    Includes index.
    For primary school age.
    Self-control—Juvenile literature.
179.9

Managing Editor: Vanessa Lanaway
Editor: Helena Newton
Proofreader: Kirstie Innes-Will
Designer: Kerri Wilson
Page layout: Pier Vido
Photo researcher: Sarah Johnson (management: Debbie Gallagher)
Production Controller: Vanessa Johnson

Printed in China

Acknowledgements
The author and the publisher are grateful to the following for permission to reproduce copyright material:

Front cover photograph: Boy doing homework, Jupiter Unlimited

Photos courtesy of:
Nancy R. Cohen/Getty Images, **4**; Steve Craft/Getty Images, **18**; Thomas Northcut/Getty Images, **6**; Stuart O'Sullivan/Getty Images, **16**; Christopher
Robbins/Getty Images, **15**; Ariel Skelley/Getty Images, **11**; Stockbyte/Getty Images, **19**; Maria Teijeiro/Getty Images, **14**; Jupiter Unlimited, **1**, **3**, **17**, **20**,
24, **26**, **27**, **28**, **30**; © Carmen Martínez Banús/iStockphoto, **8**; Alex Mares-Manton/Photolibrary, **7**; 4x5 Coll-Kevin Radford/Photolibrary, **5**; © Orange Line
Media/Shutterstock, **10**; © Monkey Business Images/Shutterstock, **25**; © jean schweitzer/Shutterstock, **21**; © kristian sekulic/Shutterstock, **13**; © Kenneth
Sponsler/Shutterstock, **9**; © Zurijeta/Shutterstock, **23**; Stockxpert, **12**, **22**, **29**.

While every care has been taken to trace and acknowledge copyright, the publisher tenders their apologies for any accidental infringement
where copyright has proved untraceable. Where the attempt has been unsuccessful, the publisher welcomes information that would redress
the situation.

For Nick, Ashley and Thomas

Contents

When a word is printed in **bold**, you can look up its meaning in the Glossary on page 31.

Values

Values are the things you believe in. They guide the way:
- you think
- you speak
- you **behave**.

Values help you to behave in a friendly way at a school camp.

Values help you to decide what is right and what is wrong. They also help you to live your life in a meaningful way.

Values help you to follow the rules when racing billycarts.

Self-discipline

Self-discipline is managing your feelings. It is trying not to shout when you feel angry. It is trying not to cry when you feel **disappointed**.

You may feel disappointed if you cannot go to a friend's party.

Self-discipline is also controlling your **behaviour**. It is doing what is right and stopping yourself from doing what is wrong.

Raising your hand instead of calling out is one way to control your behaviour.

People with self-discipline

People with self-discipline make decisions and do jobs at the right time. They do not say, 'I will think about it later,' or 'I will do it tomorrow.'

Cleaning your fish bowl each week shows self-discipline.

People with self-discipline think carefully about the **consequences** of their **behaviour**. They make good choices when they are with their family, friends and neighbours.

Getting lost is one consequence of wandering away from family members at a theme park.

Showing self-discipline with family

Family members show self-discipline by doing what needs to be done first. Then they do what they want to do. They do jobs around the home before playing or resting.

Drying the dishes before playing is being self-disciplined.

It takes self-discipline to finish a family project. You may need to spend time doing difficult or boring jobs to **achieve** something worthwhile.

Although it can take a long time to paint a doll's house, it is worth the effort.

Showing self-discipline with friends

People show self-discipline with friends by thinking for themselves. When a friend has an idea, they ask themselves, 'Is this a good idea?' Then they do what they think is right.

A person with self-discipline would tell a friend not to send mean emails.

People also show self-discipline with friends by keeping their promises. They put in the time and **effort** to do what they said they would do.

Keeping a promise to warm up with a friend before training shows self-discipline.

Showing self-discipline with neighbours

People with self-discipline are **considerate** to their neighbours. They control their **behaviour** and do not do things that might upset their neighbours.

Making sure a backyard party does not get too noisy shows consideration for neighbours.

People with self-discipline speak and behave calmly when faced with **problems** in their neighbourhood. They work with others to **solve** the problems.

Sometimes neighbours talk about where to ride their bikes safely.

Ways to show self-discipline

There are many different ways to show self-discipline with your family, friends and neighbours. Managing your feelings is a good way to start showing self-discipline.

People who manage their feelings stay calm when they are lost.

Thinking before you speak and controlling your **behaviour** are also good ways to show self-discipline. Creating **routines** will also help you to be self-disciplined.

Creating a homework routine will help you to get your homework done on time.

Managing your feelings

Managing your feelings is one way to show self-discipline. This means not shouting, breaking things or hitting others when you feel angry.
It means explaining why you feel angry.

Shouting when you feel angry shows a lack of self-discipline.

People who manage their feelings do not cry when they lose a game. They know that it is more important to be a good sport than to win.

Tennis players shake hands after a game whether they win or lose.

Thinking before you speak

Thinking before you speak is another way to show self-discipline. It is important to think about what you will say and how you will say it.

People who think before they speak always find something nice to say about a gift.

It is also important to try not to hurt other people's feelings. You cannot take back words once you have spoken.

Telling a friend that you do not like her clothing may hurt her feelings.

Controlling your behaviour

Controlling your **behaviour** is being self-disciplined. People who control their behaviour choose to behave well. They enjoy feeling happy, healthy and safe.

Controlling how much party food you eat is being self-disciplined.

Sometimes people do not have enough money to buy things that they want. They control their behaviour by not taking things that do not belong to them.

A person with self-discipline would ask before taking a friend's bubble blower.

Creating routines

Creating **routines** helps you to be self-disciplined. Routines help you to remember what you should do and when you should do it.

You will find it easier to get to sleep if you have a bedtime routine.

A good routine for getting ready for school starts with waking up on time. You then need to get dressed, eat breakfast, clean your teeth and pack your bag.

Eating breakfast is an important part of a morning routine.

Setting limits

Setting limits also helps you to be self-disciplined. People who set limits do not spend too much time on an activity or job.

Setting limits means not spending hours talking on the telephone.

People who set limits balance their lives. They do homework and jobs around the home, and still have time for fun. They also get enough rest and do enough exercise.

Watching less television means you will have more time to play outside.

Setting and working towards goals

Setting and working towards **goals** shows self-discipline. People with self-discipline decide what their goals are. Then they find out how to work towards them.

If your goal is to buy a toy, you will need to save money.

You will need to put in time and **effort** to **achieve** your goals. You may need to practise for many years to become good at playing music or sport.

Cello students practise several times a week to learn new pieces of music.

Personal set of values

There are many different values. Everyone has a personal set of values. This set of values guides people in big and little ways in their daily lives.

A swimmer needs self-discipline to train for a swimming race.

Glossary

achieve   bring about by hard work

behave   act in a certain way

consequences   results

considerate   thoughtful of other people's feelings
                     and needs

disappointed   unhappy because something you hoped would
                     happen did not happen

effort   hard work

goals   things you aim for or want to achieve

problems   things that are difficult to understand or do

routines   sets of jobs or activities, which are always
                     done in the same way

solve   find the answer to

Index